EXCEL
VLOOKUP
FORMULA
NINJA

HENRY E. MEJIA

EXCEL VLOOKUP FORMULA NINJA

Copyright © 2020 HENRY E. MEJIA

DEDICATION

To my parents, who have taught me that life is about
overcoming obstacles and enjoying it.

CONTENTS

ACKNOWLEDGMENTS

I would like to thank all those who supported me throughout the creation of this book, either with words of encouragement or with ideas to improve it.

INTRODUCTION

Welcome to a new EXCEL NINJA book! The fastest, the most practice-based and definitely the most straightforward Excel Book Series you will ever find!

You will learn to use with confidence the most important and useful Excel Formula: VLOOKUP.

Excel Ninja Series is all about this:

- **Learning fast**
- **Having fun while learning**
- **Learning trough practice (from the very beginning)**
- **No unnecessary fillers to make the book look longer**

- **The most straightforward and lean approach**
- **Getting results!**

Loaded with a gigantic amount of practice spreadsheets, examples, and recommendations.

My goal for this Excel Ninja Series was to achieve the perfect balance between a lot of exercises and examples without compromising the straightforward approach, and that's what you will find here!

That being said, I would like to summarize the benefits of becoming an Excel VLOOKUP Ninja:

- Increased chances of getting a promotion and better jobs (Because you are more productive and have better skills)
- Less workload (Excel does the heavy lifting)

- More free time
- Less stress
- A sense of growth (When you learn something new you feel great, and you know it!)
- Etc., etc.

I could spend more time, word and pages explaining to you the benefits and the importance of becoming an EXCEL VLOOKUP NINJA, but I promised that I won't fill this book with unnecessary words so let's start the first chapter right now!

GET YOUR 20 PRACTICE SPREADSHEETS (.XLSX)

Before starting Chapter 1 I recommend you to get your 20 practice spreadsheets. Those exercise files are included for everyone who purchases this book. They will serve you at the end of each chapter to reinforce what you have learned and make sure you have learned it well.

All you have to do is to send me an email to:

ems.online.empire@gmail.com

With the Subject *“VLOOKUP NINJA PRACTICE SPREADSHEETS”* and saying:

"Hello, I bought your book EXCEL VLOOKUP NINJA and I need the 20

practice spreadsheets"

I will gladly reply your email and send you the files.

Now you are ready to start Chapter 1. Let's go!

CHAPTER 1:

DATABASES

WHAT IS A DATABASE?

A database is a whole bunch of information organized in columns and rows. Normally, at your job, you have many databases.

You can have a Client database, a Sales database, Purchases database, Inventory database, and so on. Normally, those databases are exported from the ERP software to Excel, and that's when you need to show the world that you are an Excel Ninja!

Here you have an example of a mini database. You will notice that:

1. You have a label row on the top, that includes the name of each column.
2. The database is organized in columns
3. This database only has 8 rows deep. When using Vlookup your workload is the same with an 8-row database than with an 8,000-row database. Vlookup does the hard work for you.

ID	HEROE	SECTOR	CITY	BOSS
1	Superman	Healthcare	Danvers, Massachusetts	Verlie Mchenry
2	X-Men	Utilities	Canonsburg, Pennsylvania	Kiersten Thor
3	James Bond	Industrial Goods	North Chicago, Illinois	Ivey Burghardt
4	Maximus	Consumer Goods	Omaha, Nebraska	Cleta Klenke
5	Batman	Financial	Cambridge, Massachusetts	Herta Crinklaw
6	Ethan Hunt	Utilities	Richfield, Minnesota	Janel Joplin
7	Tsunade	Technology	Tysons Corner, Virginia	Cristin Hogans
8	Aquaman	Conglomerates	North Chicago, Illinois	Kenia Tandy

By the way! Did you notice that I'm using the name of many heroes in the database? That is because we are going to use them the whole book, at least that way we can practice and have fun at the same time.

You will need to use Vlookup when you have a database, and try to:

- Find specific information
- Organize information based on specific criteria
- Create a Search tool
- Grab information from multiple databases at the same time
- Many other tasks related to databases

Always remember that Databases will feed your Vlookup formula. In other words, without a Database you are not able to use a Vlookup formula.

So, basically: **Databases are your MAIN SOURCE OF INFORMATION, and VLOOKUP is a powerful tool that helps** you to obtain the correct information **FAST and EASILY!** Without being you the one that spends time finding the information manually.

QUICK CHAPTER SUMMARY

- Databases are the main source of information
- Vlookup is a powerful tool to obtain information from databases
- Databases feed Vlookup
- Vlookup does the hard work for you, so you spend almost no time getting the info you want.

CHAPTER 2:

VLOOKUP FUNCTION STRUCTURE

WHAT IS A FUNCTION?

A Function is a formula that you can use in Microsoft Excel in order to get an automatic result based on the values that you entered in that formula. So, from now on, Functions and Formulas are the same, ok?

There are lots of different functions that perform different calculations (too many of them) so learning them all is almost impossible and not time effective because you won't use them all. So, my advice to you is the next one:

1. Learn the most useful functions first (EXCEL VLOOKUP IS SO USEFUL AND FLEXIBLE THAT IT WAS BETTER TO DEDICATE A COMPLETE BOOK FOR IT)
2. Figure out which other function you need to learn in order to perform your work

You will find many of the most useful formulas in my book Excel Formulas Ninja!

"A STRAIGHTFORWARD, EXERCISE-BASED AND FAST WAY TO LEARN EXCEL FUNCTIONS" - *Employee from a State Department of Education*

As I said before, trough "Excel Vlookup Ninja" you will MASTER the Vlookup Formula and really get deep practical knowledge of it.

If you want to master Vlookup, it can't be explained in just 1 chapter, it needs to be fully explained in a complete book like this one. So, Congratulations! When you finish this book, you will be a Vlookup Ninja.

HOW CAN YOU USE FUNCTIONS IN EXCEL?

When you open an Excel spreadsheet, you will find the "Formulas" section, and then you have 2 options:

- **Option A:** Click the "Insert Function" icon and choose the function
- **Option B:** Click in the "Category" you want (Recently used, Financial, Logical, Text) and then choose the Function.

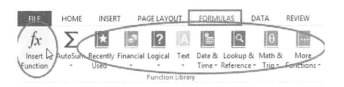

However, I don't like neither of those options because it takes too much time. **It is easier to simply click on the cell where you want to write the formula and write**

=NAMEOFTHEFUNCTION(

WHAT IS THAT? Well, every formula has its own name, that way Excel identifies what you want to do.

- Writing $=$ is the way you say to Excel that you are starting a function or formula
- The different **NamesOfTheFunctions** is what you are going to learn
- Writing **(** means that you will start to add values to the formula, so it can calculate what you want

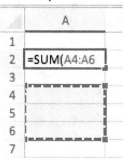

Here you can see that the Name of the function is **SUM** and the values that I'm writing are **CELLS A4, A5 and A6. (A4:A6 is the whole range or matrix involving those 3 Cells)**

Another example here. The name of the Function is **IF**, and I'm using different Cells to give an order to Excel.

That's the way we use functions.

HOW CAN I EDIT FUNCTIONS IN EXCEL?

You can do that by double clicking in the cell that has the function. That way you will be able to change the function or the values within the parenthesis.

HOW ARE FUNCTIONS STRUCTURED IN EXCEL?

Basically, any function is structured (divided) in parts, called Arguments, that are written inside the parenthesis.

=FUNCTION(Argument 1,Argument 2,Argument 3,......)

Some of the functions have just 1 argument, some of them more than one. Some of the functions have optional arguments and some of them just have mandatory arguments.

VLOOKUP STRUCTURE

Vlookup has 4 arguments (4 parts) and you need to learn them right now.

To make this explanation understandable, imagine that you have a mini database (normally they are larger, but this will do it for the example) and a search tool. You need to find the City of the Hero based on the ID.

ID	CITY
3	

ID	HERO	SECTOR	CITY
1	Krillin	Healthcare	Danvers, Massachusetts
2	Aragorn	Utilities	Canonsburg, Pennsylvania
3	Zorro	Industrial Goods	North Chicago, Illinois

1ST ARGUMENT (LOOKUP VALUE)

The first argument is the LOOKUP VALUE. This is the single most important factor in the formula because VLOOKUP will use that value to match another value inside a database. In simple words, the Lookup Value is like the anchor that you want to use to get a result that matches that anchor.

ID	CITY
3	

ID	HERO	SECTOR	CITY
1	Krillin	Healthcare	Danvers, Massachusetts
2	Aragorn	Utilities	Canonsburg, Pennsylvania

| 3 | Zorro | Industrial Goods | North Chicago, Illinois |

In the example, the LOOKUP VALUE would be the cell with the number 3. Why? Because based on that cell, we want Excel o automatically change the name of the city.

What Excel is going to do later (with the help of the remaining arguments) is to try to find inside a database the same Lookup Value.

2nd ARGUMENT (TABLE ARRAY)

The TABLE ARRAY is the Range (Group of contiguous cells) where you have your database. In this example you have the range involving 5 rows deep and involving 4 columns (the IDS, Heroes, Sectors and Cities)

ID	CITY
3	

ID	HERO	SECTOR	CITY

1	Krillin	Healthcare	Danvers, Massachusetts
2	Aragorn	Utilities	Canonsburg, Pennsylvania
3	Zorro	Industrial Goods	North Chicago, Illinois
4	Black Panther	Consumer Goods	Omaha, Nebraska
5	Catwoman	Financial	Cambridge, Massachusetts

With this argument you are telling Excel to things:

1. Where to look your Argument 1 (Lookup Value)
2. Possible results that you want to get (wait for the 3rd Argument)

SUPER IMPORTANT NOTE:

In order for VLOOKUP FORMULA to work properly, you need your LOOKUP VALUE (argument 1) to be in the FIRST

COLUMN (left column) of the **TABLE ARRAY** Range.

This is mandatory for Vlookup formula. So, in this example, if and **ID** is the Lookup Value (anchor) then the IDs must be the first column of the Table Array.

So, what happens when the Lookup Value is in the right side or in the middle of the Table Array? You have 2 options:

1. Copy and Paste the entire column in order for it to be in the left side of the Table Array
2. Use the Xlookup formula (I'll explain that in Chapter 9)

Don't worry too much right now, you'll get this better in as you move deeper in to the book.

3rd ARGUMENT (COLUMN INDEX NUMBER)

In this argument you need to specify the number of the column (from you Table Array) that has the result you want.

In the example, you want to get the name of the city. So, let's count the columns:

- ID is column 1 (from left to right)
- Name of the Hero is column 2
- Sector is column 3
- City is column 4

So, you would need to write the number 4 in the 3rd argument of the formula.

ID	CITY
3	

ID	HERO	SECTOR	CITY
1	Krillin	Healthcare	Danvers, Massachusetts
2	Aragorn	Utilities	Canonsburg, Pennsylvania

3	Zorro	Industrial Goods	North Chicago, Illinois
4	Black Panther	Consumer Goods	Omaha, Nebraska
5	Catwoman	Financial	Cambridge, Massachusetts

In that example, Excel would look for the Lookup Value (the number 3) then, Excel would try to find the number 3 INSIDE THE FIRST COLUMN OF THE TABLE ARRAY (that corresponds to Zorro) and then, Excel would return the value that is in the column number 4 (North Chicago, Illinois)

That is how the Vlookup formula makes it "thinking process". But we have one more argument to go.

4th ARGUMENT (RANGE LOOKUP)

The Range Lookup argument is optional and has nothing to do with the definition of "Range" (Group of Contiguous cells) that we already know.

Instead, this "Range Lookup" argument grants you the choice to select if you want to perform and EXACT MATCH SEARCH or an APPROXIMATE MATCH CELL

- EXACT MATCH: The Lookup Value (1st Argument) Must be exactly the same inside the database in order to get a result
- APPROXIMATE MATCH: The Lookup Value (1st Argument) can be slightly different and you would still be able to get a result, although you can get several errors in this situation.

This argument is useful when your lookup values are names.

RULE OF THUMB: ALWAYS USE EXACT MATCH

To use exact match you will need to write FALSE or 0. To use approximate match you will need to use TRUE or 1

QUICK CHAPTER SUMMARY:

- Formulas are divided in parts called arguments
- A Range is a group of Contiguous cells
- Vlookup has 4 arguments

CHAPTER 3:

BASIC USE OF VLOOKUP

It is time to start using Vlookup at its basic level. Do you remember I told you that this book had no fluff? This is when I keep my promise and start right away with the exercises! So, you are going to learn on the fly, trough practice.

EXERCISE (Open file Chapter3ex1.xlsx)

In this exercise you have a database that includes heroes IDs, Names, Industries and Cities. Also, you have a little "Search Tool" that you need to create with the help of Vlookup.

The outcome of the "Search Tool" should be this one: When you write a random number ID, the yellow cell must show the hero name that matches that ID.

13

ID	NAME	INDUSTRY	CITY
1	Captain America	Consumer Services	Toledo
2	Robin	Gas Utilities	Albuquerque
3	Captain Marvel	Information Technology	Denver
4	Picollo	Specialty Chemicals	Saint Paul
5	Batman	Health Insurance	Chula Vista

How could you do it?

Step 1: Position yourself in cell B1 to start writing the formula. Why? Because in B1 is where you want the result (Name of the hero) to show up.

And let's start writing an equal sign, the name of the formula and opening a parenthesis

=VLOOKUP(

Step 2: Remember the Arguments? This is when you need to use them. Let's start with the first argument, Lookup Value.

Ask yourself, which cell is going to be my "anchor" cell?

Based on which value my result is going to change?

If you ask yourself these questions you will figure out that the lookup value must be the cell A1, where you have a random ID, and based on that ID the formula will show a result.

13

So please, inside our formula write A1 (or select A1) and write a comma after it.

=VLOOKUP(**A1,**

Why do you need a comma? Because those commas are the ones that separate the arguments. Without them, Excel wouldn't know which argument is the first or the second.

Step 3: Now you need the 2nd Argument, the Table Array. Remember that the Table Array is the Range where your database is found, and its first columns MUST be the ID column. Why? Because you are using IDs as the lookup value, and remember that the lookup value MUST be founded in the first column of your Table Array.

Ask yourself, where is my complete database?

You will find that your database is found from A3 to D32. It includes the following:

- From A3 to A32
- From B3 to B32
- From C3 to C32

- From D3 to D32

That is why the range is A3:D32

So please, inside our formula that range and write a comma after it.

=VLOOKUP(A1,A3:D32,

Step 4: Now you need the 3rd Argument, the Column Index Number. This one is easy but a little bit tricky.

Identify your Table Array and ask yourself: In which column (from left to right) is the result I want?

Remember that you want to get the name of the hero by writing a random ID. So, **in which column of your Table Array are the names?**

1   2   3   4

ID NAME INDUSTRY CITY

The answer is "In column number 2". That's the number you need in your 3rd argument. Go ahead and write it, followed by a comma.

=VLOOKUP(A1,A3:D32,2,

Step 5: The last argument is the easiest one, as I told you before. You just need to write 0 or FALSE. That way Excel will perform an "Exact Search".

So, your Lookup value MUST be written exactly the same in the database as in the Lookup Value cell in order to get a result. In this example, there is no problem because the lookup values are numbers, is hard to write them incorrectly.

With this last Argument, you won't need a comma, but you will need to close the parenthesis to show Excel that you have finished your formula. Lastly, press Enter.

=VLOOKUP(**A1,A3:D32,2,FALSE**)

3	Captain Marvel

ID	NAME	INDUSTRY	CITY
1	Captain America	Consumer Services	Toledo
2	Robin	Gas Utilities	Albuquerque
3	Captain Marvel	Information Technology	Denver
4	Picollo	Specialty Chemicals	Saint Paul

You can notice that you get the result automatically. Also, if you change the ID number in the lookup value, you will get the correct result instantaneously.

13	Obi Wan Kenobi

ID	NAME	INDUSTRY	CITY
1	Captain America	Consumer Services	Toledo
2	Robin	Gas Utilities	Albuquerque
13	Obi Wan Kenobi	Application Software	Raleigh
14	Jack Sparrow	Property Insurance	Atlanta
15	Supergirl	Semiconductor - Broad Line	Seattle

That's how you use Vlookup at a basic level.

MORE EXERCISES

Now is time for you to solve a similar exercise by yourself.

Chapter3ex2.xlsx

Chapter3ex3.xlsx

Chapter3ex4.xlsx

QUICK CHAPTER SUMMARY:

- Remember to ask yourself the questions I gave you when trying to figure out the Vlookup Arguments.
- The Lookup Value (1st argument) is the anchor
- The Table Array is the database
- Column Index Number is the number of the column where the result you want is.

Are you enjoying this book?

Do you think it's easy to understand?

Have the exercises helped you learn faster?

Without knowing your opinion, I won't know if the book has helped you to become a better Excel user.

You can share your thoughts with me by writing a Review

CHAPTER 4

DRAGGING FORMULAS (ABSOLUTE REFERENCES)

Dragging formulas is a natural part of using Excel. It is useful because you can "replicate" formulas in contiguous cells without having to write the whole formula again.

Look at the following picture. Imagine you need to get 4 different results (for each one of the IDs there). It would be time consuming if you want to write the formula 4 times! In that situation you can DRAG the formula down and replicate the exact same formula 4 times.

ID	INDUSTRY
5	
10	
15	
20	

But we face one little problem, all the formula arguments would be dragged down too! And that is a problem because, do you remember the Table Array range (The database)? That range must not move at all.

So that is where Absolute References are important. An Absolute Reference is used to "fix" or "immobilize" any argument (or all of them) according to our needs.

HOW DO I RECOGNIZE AN ABSOLUTE REFERENCE?

Absolute references in Excel are recognized because they have dollar signs **($)**

next to the letter or number of a cell, inside a formula.

=**VLOOKUP($A$1,** Would mean that, no matter where I drag the formula, the first argument is ALWAYS going to be A1, because is immobilized with Absolute References

=**VLOOKUP($A1,** Would mean that, if I drag the formula down, the first argument WILL move down (A2 or A3 or A4), because we didn't immobilize the row number (1). But, if we drag the formula to the right or the left, the first argument will be kept at the A column, because that column is immobilized. (This is called "Relative Reference")

=**VLOOKUP(A$1,** Would mean that the first argument will always be in row 1, but it can be moved to another column. (Also "Relative Reference")

=**VLOOKUP(A1,** Would mean that the first argument will always be moved as you drag the formula because you have not immobilized it.

HOW CAN I INSERT ABSOLUTE REFERENCES?

Option 1: Writing the dollar signs manually inside the formula

Option 2: Clicking inside the formula and inside the argument you want to immobilize and:

> For Mac users: Cmd + T

> For Windows users: F4

Now let's try an exercise!

EXERCISE (Open file Chapter4ex1.xlsx)

You have a similar exercise to the previous one, but the main difference is that now you need to get 4 results fast!

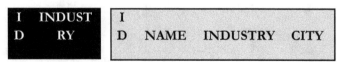

ID	INDUSTRY		ID	NAME	INDUSTRY	CITY

5		1	Captain America	Consumer Services	Toledo
10		2	Robin	Gas Utilities	Albuquerque
1		3	Captain Marvel	Information Technology	Denver
2		4	Picollo	Specialty Chemicals	Saint Paul
		5	Batman	Health Insurance	Chula Vista
		6	The Rocketeer	Insurance Brokers	St Louis

Step 1: Position yourself in cell B3 to start writing the formula.

=VLOOKUP(

Step 2: Ask yourself, which cell is going to be my "anchor" cell? Based on which value my result is going to change?

The first ID Value is in cell A3

=VLOOKUP(**A3,**

41

Step 3: Now you need the 2nd Argument, the Table Array. Ask yourself, where is my complete database? You will find that your database is found from D2 to G31

=VLOOKUP(A1,D2:G31,

Step 4: Now you need the 3rd Argument, the Column Index Number. Identify your Table Array and ask yourself: In which column (from left to right) is the result I want?

1	2	3	4
ID	**NAME**	**INDUSTRY**	**CITY**

The answer is "In column number "3". That's the number you need in your 3rd argument.

=VLOOKUP(A1,A3:D32,3,

Step 5: You just need to write 0 or FALSE. That way Excel will perform an "Exact

Search".

=VLOOKUP(A1,A3:D32,3,FALSE)

ID	INDUSTRY
5	Health Insurance
10	
1	
2	

You got the result for the cell where you wrote the formula. Now you need to drag the formula down.

HOW CAN DRAG THE FORMULA DOWN?

Select the cell that has the formula and you will see a little dot in the bottom right corner. You need to click, hold and drag down.

Drag the formula down and you will get the following results:

ID	INDUSTRY
5	Health Insurance
10	Chemicals - Major Diversified
1	#N/A
2	#N/A

What happened? Remember that I told you that when you don't immobilize the Table Array (with absolute references) the range will be dragged down in conjunction with the formula.

	A	B	C	D	E	F	G
1							
2	**ID**	**INDUSTRY**		**ID**	**NAME**	**INDUSTRY**	**CITY**
3	5	Health Insurance		1	Captain America	Consumer Services	Toledo
4	10	Chemicals - Major Diversified		2	Robin	Gas Utilities	Albuquerque
5	1	#N/A		3	Captain Marvel	Information Technology	Denver
6	⚠	=BUSCARV(A6,D5:G34,3,0)		4	Picollo	Specialty Chemicals	Saint Paul
7				5	Batman	Health Insurance	Chula Vista

What you need to do is to add Absolute References to the Table Array argument (3rd Argument)

Step 6: Double click the formula in B3, then click the Table Array Argument (3rd argument) and Add Absolute References.

IMPORTANT NOTE: For the Table Array you need to Add Absolute References to A3 and D32 (2 absolute references in the 3rd argument)

Option 1: Write them Manually

Option 2: Cmd + T for Mac users, or F4 for Windows users

The formula now looks like this!

=VLOOKUP(A1,$A$3:$D$32,3,FALSE)

Why we didn't need to add Absolute references to the 1st argument? Because we want it to move with the formula. The only argument we want to immobilize is the 3rd argument (database).

Step 7: Drag the formula down

ID	INDUSTRY
5	Health Insurance
10	Chemicals - Major Diversified
1	Consumer Services
2	Gas Utilities

Excellent! That's how you use Absolute References!

MORE EXERCISES

Now is time for you to solve a similar exercise by yourself.

Chapter4ex2.xlsx

Chapter4ex3.xlsx

QUICK CHAPTER SUMMARY:

- Absolute References serve to "immobilize" arguments within a formula
- They are represented by dollars signs $
- They are needed every time you want to drag a formula.

CHAPTER 5

VLOOKUP WITH MULTIPLE SPREADSHEETS

You have learned a lot of things fast so far. Just to summarize a little bit of them, here they are:

- Introduction to formulas
- Vlookup Arguments
- Basic use of Vloookup
- Dragging the Vlookup Formula using Absolute references

Now it is time to use Vlookup trough different worksheets. There will be some times when a database is going to be in another worksheet from the file, and you need to know how to handle that situation.

Don't worry, the process is similar, but you will learn the single most important feature that you need to be aware of in order to build the formula correctly. Let's go to the exercise.

EXERCISE (Open file Chapter5ex1.xlsx)

In order to make it even more understandable, we are going to use a similar exercise to the previous one, with one main difference: The database is in a separate worksheet of that file.

You have a set of ID numbers and you need to get the names. Also, after writing the formula, if you change the ID numbers manually you need to watch the names change automatically

ID	NAME
5	
10	
1	
2	

Step 1: Position yourself in cell B3 to start writing the formula.

=VLOOKUP(

Step 2: Ask yourself, which cell is going to be my "anchor" cell? Based on which value my result is going to change? The first ID Value is in cell A3

=VLOOKUP(A3,

Step 3: Now you need the 2nd Argument, the Table Array. Here is where the trick is:

- Right after you write the first comma in the previous step (In other words, you need to be writing or modifying the formula for this step to work), you need to CLICK the "DATABASE" tab and THEN select the Table Array

EXERCISE	DATABASE

The range of the database is from B2 to E31. So it is B2:E31. But you will notice something different: The Table Array is shown like this

=VLOOKUP(A3,DATABASE!B2:E31

WHY? Because it means that the Table Array is going to be taken from the worksheet in your file called "DATABASE". In fact you can change the name of that worksheet to "TEST" and the formula would look like this

=VLOOKUP(A3,TEST!B2:E31

IMPORTANT NOTE: EVERYTIME YOU TAKE A CELL (AS AN ARGUMENT) THAT IS IN ANOTHER WORKSHEET, THE FORMULA WILL

ADD IN THAT ARGUMENT THE NAME OF THE WORKSHEET AND A (!) SYMBOL.

So, the formula until this step is the following, and you already know why.

=VLOOKUP(A3,DATABASE!B2:E31,

Step 4: Don't forget to add Absolute References to the Table Array. It works exactly the same as the previous chapter! If you forget to add absolute references, when you drag the formula the Table Array is going to be moved away.

=VLOOKUP(A3,DATABASE!$B$2:$E$31,

Step 5: Now you need the 3rd Argument, the Column Index Number. Identify your Table Array and ask yourself: In which column (from left to right) is the result I want?

1	2	3	4

ID	NAME	INDUSTRY	CITY

The answer is "In column number "2". That's the number you need in your 3rd argument.

=VLOOKUP(A3,DATABASE!$B$2:$E$31,2,

Step 6: You just need to write 0 or FALSE. That way Excel will perform an "Exact Search". Close the parenthesis, press enter and drag the formula down!

=VLOOKUP(A3,DATABASE!$B$2:$E$31,2,0)

ID	NAME
5	Batman
10	The Incredibles
1	Captain America
2	Robin

Step 7: Go ahead, change the ID numbers to confirm that your formula works fine in every one of the 4 cells.

ID	NAME
10	The Incredibles
15	Supergirl
20	James Bond
25	Marvelman

That's the way you use Vlookup trough different worksheets!

MORE EXERCISES

Now is time for you to solve a similar exercise by yourself.

Chapter5ex2.xlsx

Chapter5ex3.xlsx

QUICK CHAPTER SUMMARY:

- The use of Vlookup with different worksheets is just a little bit trickier
- Remember that the formula will contain "NAMEOFTHEWORKSHEET"! in the argument that was taken from another worksheet
- Remember to Add absolute references when needed

CHAPTER 6

ERRORS WHEN USING VLOOKUP AND HOW TO FIX THEM

This is the chapter where you are going to learn about the errors you may find when you use Vlookup formula.

The purpose of Excel showing an Error to you is to warn you that something in your formula is incorrect and needs to be fixed.

You will find 4 kinds of Errors:

#NAME! ERROR

This error happens basically when you write the name of the formula incorrectly. As an example, instead of writing

=VLOOKUP

You write something like

=VLOKUP or =VLOOKUB or =BLOOKUP

To solve this error you need to modify the name of the formula.

#N/A ERROR

This error shows up when Excel couldn't find your lookup value (1st argument) in the first column of your Table Array (2nd Argument).

Probable cause 1: The lookup value is not in the Table Array

Probable cause 2: The lookup value is slightly written different in the Table Array

To solve this error:

Option 1: Change the 4th Argument to TRUE, so you can find and Approximate Match, just in case the lookup value is written different

Option 2: Search and Find manually in the Table Array to confirm that your lookup value is there

Option 3: Double Check your Table Array (2nd Argument) in order to confirm that its first column is in the same column as the lookup value is.

#REF! ERROR

This error appears in 2 situations:

Situation 1: The lookup value cell was eliminated from the spreadsheet. When you right-click and select delete cell, you can activate this error if the cell you are deleting is the one with the lookup value. But this error is not common. The most common #REF! error is the next one.

Situation 2: The column index number (3rd argument) has a column number that doesn't exists in your Table Array (2nd Argument).

Example, if your Table Array is A1:B10 you have 2 columns, but if your Column Index Number (3rd argument) has a 3, then you are searching for a column that doesn't exists in your Table Array, and Excel gives you a #REF!

#VALUE! ERROR

The easiest one. Normally when you have this error the problem is in the Column Index Number argument and is because you wrote a 0 or a negative number on it.

If you have this error, go directly and check the Column index number.

EXERCISE (Open file Chapter6ex1.xlsx)

Let's start with this exercise. We have a search tool and a Database. As you may see, there are 4 different errors. Our mission is to find the mistakes and correct them.

NAME	CITY TO SAVE
Aquaman	#¿NAME?
Batgirl	#¡REF!
Ant Man	#N/A
Black Panther	#¡VALUE!

Step 1: Position yourself in cell B3 and observe the formula.

=VLOKUP(A3,$D$2:$G$89,2,0)

The error you have is the NAME error so, something must be wrong with the name of the formula **VLOKUP**. Double click on B3 to modify the formula

=VLOOKUP(A3,$D$2:$G$89,2,0)

And that's it!

Step 2: Position yourself in cell B4 and observe the formula.

=VLOOKUP(A4,$D$2:$G$89,5,0)

The error you have is the REF error so, something must be wrong with the Column Index Number. You will see that the Column Index Number is 5, but the Table Array just have 4 columns.

| 1 | 2 | 3 | 4 |

NAME	CITY TO SAVE	2020 POPULATION	2019 POPULATION

You need to correct that mistake. Double click on B3 to modify the formula

=VLOOKUP(A4,$D$2:$G$89,2,0)

Step 3: Position yourself in cell B5 and observe the formula.

=VLOOKUP(A5,$D$2:$G$89,2,0)

Everything in the formula looks fine. The error you have is the N/A error so, something must be wrong with the lookup value or the Table Array. You will see that **"Ant Man"** (lookup value) is written **"Ant-Man"** in the Table Array. So, when you modify the lookup value adding the middle "-" to the name, you will get the correct result.

Step 4: Position yourself in cell B6 and observe the formula.

=VLOOKUP(A6,$D$2:$G$89,0,0)

The error you have is the VALUE error so, something must be wrong with the Column Index Number. You will see that the Column Index Number is 0, that's not possible, so change that number.

=VLOOKUP(A6,$D$2:$G$89,2,0)

NAME	CITY TO SAVE
Aquaman	Delhi
Batgirl	Dhaka
Ant-Man	Tokyo

Black Panther	Osaka

And that's how you deal with the Vlookup Errors that you may find sometimes.

MORE EXERCISES

Now is time for you to solve a similar exercise by yourself.

Chapter6ex2.xlsx

Chapter6ex2.xlsx

QUICK CHAPTER SUMMARY:

- ERRORS are common when using Vlookup and you need to handle them.
- There are 4 types of error, and each one of them has its own causes.
- Table Array, Column Index number and differently written lookup values are the most common causes of errors.

CHAPTER 7

IFERROR + VLOOKUP (COMBINED FORMULAS)

Sometimes, you will know that you will get errors (normally N/A Errors) because you are sure your database is missing some of the values. When you face this situation and you want to get rid of the annoying errors, you can use the formula IFERROR.

WHAT IS IFERROR FUNCTION FOR?

Basically, is a formula that allows you to choose your own custom the result in case you get an error (So you don't get an ugly #N/A in your search tool).

The important feature with this formula is

that it needs to be NESTED (Combined) with the Vlookup Formula.

WHAT IS A NESTED FORMULA?

A nested formula (combined formula) is a formula INSIDE another formula!

How can this be done? If you insert one formula inside an argument of another formula, then you have a NESTED FORMULA! And it looks like this)

=MAINFORMULA1(NESTEDFORMULA(argument1,argument2),argument2)

- Notice that the first formula starts the same. With an equal sign, the name of the formula, open parenthesis
- The NESTED FORMULA does no need an equal sign. It just needs to be written as if it were an argument. In the example above, the NESTEDFORMULA took the role of

the argument 1 of the MAINFORMULA.

- Also notice that you need to close the parenthesis of the nested formula before starting to write the second argument of the MAINFORMULA.

So, that's how a nested formula is structured.

HOW IS THE IFERROR FORMULA STRUCTURED?

IFERROR has 2 arguments:

=IFERROR(value,value if error)

- VALUE: This is the value (or formula) we would normally want to get if we don't get any errors.
- VALUE IF ERROR: This is the vale (or formula) we would want to get IF WE GET AN ERROR.

Let's try this with an exercise.

EXERCISE (Open file Chapter7ex1.xlsx)

Let's start with this exercise. We have a search tool with the name of our heroes and we want to know the money the will receive in their bank accounts. (Yes, they need money too).

NAME	EARNINGS
The Atom	
X-Men	
Asterix	
Maximus	
Conan the Barbarian	
Ethan Hunt	

And we also have a database with the earnings from the last week. BUT YOU WILL FIND THAT NOT EVERY HERO WORKED THE LAST WEEK! They were lazy!

If you perform a straight Vlookup search you will get a lot of #N/A errors (You can try it).

NAME	EARNINGS FROM LAST WEEK
X-Men	7,642,147
Asterix	27,058,479
Sub-Mariner	9,304,016
Itachi Uchiha	4,443,186

So now, we are going to use the Combined IFERROR and VLOOKUP formulas.

IMPORTANT NOTE: The VLOOKUP FORMULA IS GOING TO BE INSIDE THE IFERROR FORMULA.

Step 1: Position yourself in cell B3 and start writing the IFERROR formula and open a parenthesis.

=IFERROR(

Step 2: The 1st argument of IFERROR is "The value that we want to get if there is no error". That means that we need to write the VLOOKUP formula in that argument.

Why? Because if there is no error, we want Excel to perform Vlookup as it normally would.

So, start writing the VLOOKUP formula and the and open another parenthesis.

NOTE: The first opened parenthesis was IFERROR's opening. The second is VLOOKUP's opening.

=IFERROR(VLOOKUP(

Step 3: Write the Lookup Value (1st argument) of VLOOKUP, in this case, A3

=IFERROR(VLOOKUP(A3,

Step 4: Write the Table Array (2nd argument) of Vlookup, in this case D2:E32, and

REMEMBER TO ADD ABSOLUTE REFERENCES!

=IFERROR(VLOOKUP(A3,$D$2:$E$32,

Step 5: Write the Column Index Number (3rd argument) of Vlookup, in this case 2.

=IFERROR(VLOOKUP(A3,$D$2:$E$32, 2,

Step 6: Write 0 or FALSE in the 4th argument of Vlookup AND CLOSE THE PARENTHESIS. Remember that this closed parenthesis is for VLOOKUP formula, not for IFERROR, because the IFERROR formula continues.

=IFERROR(VLOOKUP(A3,$D$2:$E$32, 2,0)

Step 7: Write a comma. This comma is to separate the IFERROR's first argument (that is a complete vlookup function) of the second IFERROR's argument.

=IFERROR(VLOOKUP(A3,$D$2:$E$32, 2,0),

Step 7: Write the VALUE IF ERROR (2nd argument of IFERROR). In this situation we want Excel to write "DID NOT WORK" to the heroes that deliver a #N/A error.

You need to write that between "". Like this
"DID NOT WORK"

Lastly, close the parenthesis, press enter and drag the formula down!

=IFERROR(VLOOKUP(A3,$D$2:$E$32, 2,0),"DID NOT WORK")

NAME	EARNINGS
The Atom	DID NOT WORK
X-Men	7642147
Asterix	27058479

Maximus	DID NOT WORK
Conan the Barbarian	DID NOT WORK
Ethan Hunt	DID NOT WORK

Notice how, instead of getting #N/A errors, you get the customized text of your choice.

This is how you use IFERROR + VLOOKUP as a Combined formula.

MORE EXERCISES

Now is time for you to solve a similar exercise by yourself.

Chapter7ex2.xlsx

QUICK CHAPTER SUMMARY:

- A nested formula is a combined formula of 2 or more functions

- A formula needs to be placed inside another formula's argument in order to create a nested formula
- The purpose of IFERROR is to give a customized text as a result in case you get an error.

CHAPTER 8

IF + VLOOKUP
(COMBINED FORMULAS)

In this chapter you are going to learn about the most powerful logical formula. The IF Formula.

IMPORTANT NOTE: THE IF FORMULA IS SO USEFUL AND POWERFUL THAT I HAVE CREATED A WHOLE BOOK FOR YOU TO MASTER THAT FORMULA AND OTHER LOGICAL FORMULAS AS WELL. TAKE A LOOK AT IT.

"The book was engaging and encouraging by providing many examples and exercises. I will eagerly study the other books in the series."

Now, let's continue with this chapter. We are going to learn to use the IF Formula in conjunction with 2 nested Vlookup formulas! Similar to what we did the last chapter, but now you will have 2 nested Vlookup functions.

The main purpose of the **IF FORMULA** is to perform a logical test and after that, return a solution based on the result of the logical test

The main benefit of this formula is that it is flexible that will return a result based on a previous logical test.

In plain English, if the logical test is TRUE, then you get one result (I could be a nested formula), if the logical test is FALSE, you get another result (it could be another nested formula).

HOW IS THE IF FUNCTION STRUCTURED?

The syntax (Structure) of the **IF** function is the next one:

=if(logical test, value if true, value if false)

WHAT DOES THAT MEAN?

LOGICAL TEST The test you want to perform in order to know if it is true or false

VALUE IF TRUE: If the logical test is met (TRUE), then this result will be shown.

VALUE IF FALSE: If the logical test is NOT met (FALSE), then this result will be shown.

Let's try an exercise.

EXERCISE (Open file Chapter8ex1.xlsx)

Our heroes took a certification exam, so they can continue to work as heroes. If they fail the exam they need to stop working until they pass the exam. But also, there some heroes that have not paid the fee! (Yes, they took the exam and they didn't pay)

STUDENT	GRADES	PAYMENT STATUS
Ben-Hur	92	PAID
Black Canary	73	OVERDUE
Sub-Mariner	41	PAID
Itachi Uchiha	54	PAID
7-800	42	PAID

Terminator		
Optimus Prime	69	OVERDUE

So, you need to create a dual Search Tool:

- If a CODE cell has the word PAYMENT, then the Search Tool needs to show the payment status.
- If the CODE cell doesn't have the word PAYMENT, then the Search Tool needs to show the grades.

CODE	

HERO	RESULT
Aragorn	
Ant-Man	
Storm	
Vegeta	

Green Lantern	
Indiana Jones	

NOTE: REMEMBER THAT 2 VLOOKUPS ARE GOING TO BE NESTED INSIDE THE IF FUNCTION. ONE VLOOKUP IS GOINT TO TAKE THE PLACE OF THE 2nd IF ARGUMENT, AND THE OTHER VLOOKUP IS GOING TO TAKE THE PLACE OF THE 3rd IF ARGUMENT.

Step 1: Position yourself in C4 and start writing the first formula.

=IF(

Step 2: Write the 1st argument of IF. Remember that your logical test needs to order Excel the following: **"IF B1 is equal to (or contains) the word PAYMENT then..."**

How? Well, we need to use any of these symbols = < > in conjunction with the cells.

First, you need to find out WHERE is the word "PAYMENT" going to be written: In B1

Then, you need to think about the logical test:

To say equal to the word PAYMENT we would write: ="PAYMENT"

To say equal to 70 we would write: =70

To say greater than 70 we would write: >70

To say equal or greater than 70 we would write: >=70

To say smaller than 70 we would write: <70

To say equal or smaller than 70 we would write: <=70

So, to say "IF B1 is equal (or contains) the word PAYMENT we would write:

=IF($B$1="PAYMENT",

NOTE: REMEMBER TO ADD ABSOLUTE REFERENCES TO B1. WHY? BECAUSE WE ARE GOING TO DRAG THE FORMULA AND WE NEED THE LOGICAL TEST TO BE ALWAYS PERFORMED WITH THE CODE CELL (B1)

Step 3: Write the 2nd IF Argument (VALUE IF TRUE) to set a result if the logical test is TRUE.

We want Excel to automatically perform a VLOOKUP formula to find the payment status B1 says "PAYMENT". So, the only thing you have to do is to write a normal NESTED VLOOKUP formula in this 2nd Argument.

=IF($B$1="PAYMENT",**VLOOKUP(B4, $E$3:$G$32,3,0),**

Explanation about the first Vlookup nested

formula

Why **B4**? Because that's the lookup value for the formula in C4

Why **$E$3:$G$32**? Because that's the Table Array (Database). And the absolute references are needed in order not to move the table Array when you drag the formula.

Why **3** in column index number? Because the column number 3 in the Table Array is "Payment Status", that's what we want to get if the logical test is TRUE (If B1 is equal to the word PAYMENT)

Why **0**? Because we want an Exact Match

Step 4: Write the 3rd IF Argument (VALUE IF FALSE) to set a result if the logical test is FALSE.

We want Excel to automatically perform a VLOOKUP formula to find the GRADES if B1 DOES NOT SAY "PAYMENT". So, the only thing you have to do is to write another NESTED VLOOKUP formula in this 3rd Argument.

=IF($B$1="PAYMENT",VLOOKUP(B4, $E$3:$G$32,3,0), VLOOKUP(B4,$E$3:$G$32,2,0)

Notice that it is almost the same Vlookup than the previous one, the only difference is in the COLUMN INDEX NUMBER: The second VLOOKUP has a Column Index Number of **2**. Why? Because the column number 2 in the Table Array are the GRADES, and that's the result we want if the logical test is FALSE (if B1 does not have the word PAYMENT).

Step 5: Finally, close the parenthesis of the IF formula. Notice that at the end of the formula you have 2 closing parenthesis, that is because one is to close the second Vlookup formula and the last one is to close the complete IF Formula.

Press enter and drag the formula down!

=IF($B$1="PAYMENT",VLOOKUP(B4,

$E$3:$G$32,3,0),
VLOOKUP(B4,$E$3:$G$32,2,0))

Notice that if you write PAYMENT, you get the payment status.

HERO	RESULT
Aragorn	OVERDUE
Ant-Man	OVERDUE
Storm	PAID
Vegeta	OVERDUE
Green Lantern	PAID
Indiana Jones	PAID

And if you erase the word PAYMENT, you get the grades automatically!

CODE

HERO	RESULT
Aragorn	35
Ant-Man	68
Storm	54
Vegeta	53
Green Lantern	91
Indiana Jones	48

This is how you can use IF Function + Vlookup combined!

MORE EXERCISES

Now is time for you to solve a similar exercise by yourself.

Chapter8ex2.xlsx

QUICK CHAPTER SUMMARY:

- The IF Formula is the most powerful logical formula
- It is so flexible that I created a complete book to fully explain that one and other logical formulas
- You can use Nested Vlookup formulas in conjunction with IF

CHAPTER 9

BASIC USE OF THE NEW XLOOKUP FORMULA

IMPORTANT AVAILABILITY NOTE

Depending on the date you are reading this, it will be the availability that XLOOKUP has in the Market.

If you read this before July 2020, then you have 2 options to practice with XLOOKUP:

1. Have an Office 365 Business Plan account (Monthly Channel) with which you will already have availability of XLOOKUP

2. Open a free Outlook account to be able to use "Excel on the Web", since XLOOKUP is also enabled there. This second option is the best in case you don't

have the Office 365 Business Plan.

In this chapter you are going to learn about the most powerful logical formula. The XLOOKUP Formula.

IMPORTANT NOTE: I HAVE CREATED A WHOLE BOOK FOR YOU TO FULLY MASTER THAT FORMULA

TAKE A LOOK AT IT.

"THIS NEW FORMULA MAKES IT EVEN EASIER THAN EXCEL VLOOKUP FUNCTION" - Manager of a Retail Chain Store

Now, let's continue with this chapter. Xlookup works almost the same as Vlookup but it has one important feature that Vlookup don't: Xlookup can search from right to left. In other words, Your Lookup Value could be at the right side of your database and you would still be able to perform the search.

WHICH ARE THE XLOOKUP ARUMENTS?

XLOOKUP has 6 arguments, but for the basic use you will only need 3 of them.

FIRST ARGUMENT: LOOKUP VALUE

This is the lookup value (just as Vlookup)

SECOND ARGUMENT LOOKUP ARRAY:

This is the Range where your Lookup values are. With Vlookup you needed to pick just 1 range. With XLOOKUP you will need to select the range where your lookup values are, and another range for the 3rd argument.

This is the reason why it doesn't matter if your lookup values are in the righ side, middle or left side of the database, because you select an independent range for them

THIRD ARGUMENT RETURN ARRAY:

Similar to the 2nd argument, you will need to select the range where your desired results are.

So, let's try the final exercise of this book to understand the Xlookup formula!

EXERCISE (Open file Chapter9ex1.xlsx)

You are facing an exercise that is similar to the one in the Chapter 4. You will need to get the name based on the IDs. The problem is that with Vlookup is impossible to do this because your lookupvalue (ID) is at the right side of the database. This is one of the situations when you use Xlookup.

ID	NAME
5	
10	
1	
2	

NAME	INDUSTRY	CITY	ID
Captain America	Consumer Services	Toledo	1
Robin	Gas Utilities	Albuquerque	2
Captain Marvel	Technology	Denver	3
Picollo	Specialty Chemicals	Saint Paul	4
Batman	Health Insurance	Chula Vista	5
The Rocketeer	Insurance Brokers	St Louis	6

| Superman | Electrical Equipment | Plano | 7 |

Step 1: Position yourself in B3 and start writing the first formula.

=XLOOKUP(

Step 2: Select your Lookup value

=XLOOKUP(A3,

Step 3: Write the 2nd argument Lookup Array. Remember that you will need to select the range (in the database) where the possible lookup values are. In this case you have them in column D from row 2 to 31. So the range is G2:G31 AND REMEMBER TO ADD ABSOLUTE REFERENCES

=XLOOKUP(A3,$G$2:$G$31,

Step 4: Write the 3rd argument Return Array. Remember that you will need to select the range (in the database) where the possible results are. In this case you have them in column G from row 2 to 31. So the range is

D2:D31 AND REMEMBER TO ADD ABSOLUTE REFERENCES, close the parenthesis, click enter and drag the formula down!

=XLOOKUP(A3,$G$2:$G$31,$D$2:$D$31)

ID	NAME
5	Batman
10	The Incredibles
1	Captain America
2	Robin

IMPORTANT NOTE: The arguments 2 and 3 need to be the same height of rows, and the top and bottom rows needs to be same in both arguments. In the exercise, G2 and D2 are the top rows in arguments 2 and 3. Also, G31 and D31 are the bottom rows. That's how you need to do it when you use Xlookup.

CONGRATULATIONS! You have finished the book and you are now an Excel Vlookup Ninja! Go ahead with the Quick Final Tips.

MORE EXERCISES

Now is time for you to solve a similar exercise by yourself.

Chapter9ex2.xlsx

Chapter9ex3.xlsx

QUICK CHAPTER SUMMARY:

- The Xlookup formula is great to search from right to left
- Is flexible and it will help you a lot at your job
- If you learn to use Vlookup and Xlookup you will easily tackle any database you have.

CHAPTER 10

QUICK FINAL TIPS

CONGRATULATIONS!! You finished the exercises and now you are an EXCEL VLOOKUP NINJA! It was a great journey.

This book wouldn't be complete without a series of final recommendations that can help you even more

Here (in this short chapter) I can't teach you everything I'm going to recommend because they are extensive topics that would not fit in a few pages, it is also information that I teach deeply in other Excel books.

However, I want to make the following recommendations you with the hope that you recognize the main tools that you must learn to be an EXCEL NINJA.

WHY DO YOU NEED TO LEARN MORE FUNCTIONS?

There are hundreds of functions that can help you to better perform your work, however you may not know them. Sometimes a new function that you learn can save you hours of weekly work in the office.

The important thing to remember about functions is that they tend to relate to each other and become stronger tools when combined or in the form of nested formulas.

I'll give you an example you already know: VLOOKUP. The VLOOKUP function is quite strong and useful on its own, but when you learned to use IF together with VLOOKUP, three things happened:

1) You learned a new function: VLOOKUP

2) You learned a new function: IF

3) You learned a new tool: IF + VLOOKUP

When you learn just two functions you actually have three tools in your toolbox. That is, your tools are not just the number of functions you master, but also include the combinations you can make between those functions.

So the more functions you know, the more combinations you can make and the more chances you have to become an Excel Champion.

That is why I created Excel Formulas Ninja! The purpose of Formulas Ninja is to teach you the TOP Formulas in Excel in an Easy and Fast Way!

Get your copy of Excel Formulas Ninja!

"A STRAIGHTFORWARD, EXERCISE-BASED AND FAST WAY TO LEARN EXCEL FUNCTIONS" - *Employee from a State Department of Education*

"The book was engaging and encouraging by providing many examples and exercises. I will eagerly study the other books in the series."

WHY DO YOU NEED TO LEARN KEYBOARD PIVOT TABLES?

Pivot Tables are the go-to tools for advanced data analysis! Whenever you are immersed in a gigantic amount of data and you need to take decisions based on that data, Pivot Tables are the way to go!

You can summarize thousands of rows and columns (literally thousands) in just a few seconds. You also can shape your summary to every imaginable way, in order to get relevant insight about your data.

Base your decisions in facts, not opinions! Buy your Pivot Tables Champion copy!

"THIS BOOK IS SO GREAT! NOW I CAN ANALYZE GIANT DATABASES WITHIN SECONDS!" - *Sales Coordinator of a Wholesale Company.*

WHY DO YOU NEED TO LEARN CONDITIONAL FORMATTING?

You will agree that the human eye identifies faster the colors and shapes than numbers. For the same reason, traffic lights have colors instead of numbers or words.

The conditional formatting in Excel is

used to add colors or shapes when certain conditions are met, making the data user-friendly and giving the opportunity to recognize patterns within the data.

Imagine for a moment that you have a table with 100 data and you need to find the values that are closest to the average.

Option 1: The first option is to use the AVERAGE function and then manually search for those values within the table.

Option 2: The fastest and easiest option is to use Conditional Format so that Excel automatically colors the data that is closest to the average, and that's it, you'll have the data you need highlighted in the color you want in a few seconds, it doesn't matter if your table has 100, 1000 or 10000 numbers.

If you would like to search for the 10 highest values within a table, you can do so. If you would like to focus only on data that is less than the average, you can color them automatically. If you want to identify the data that are between 2 values, you can do it in less than 30 seconds.

That is why I recommend conditional formatting. Becoming a Conditional Formatting Champion will allow you to find the most relevant information.

Get your copy of Conditional Formatting Champion!

"THIS GREAT AND EASY TO UNDERSTAND BOOK TEACHES A VERY USEFUL WAY TO ANALYZE DATA" - *Accounting Manager of a Sportswear Company*

WHY DO YOU NEED TO LEARN KEYBOARD SHORTCUTS?

First of all I want to recommend that you learn Excel keyboard shortcuts. Keyboard shortcuts are the easiest and fastest way to increase your productivity in Excel. You can easily cut your work time in half.

The reality is that there are more than 100 keyboard shortcuts. My recommendation is that you learn the 10 or 20 main ones. Which are the main ones? The ones you use the most depending the kind of work you have to do in Excel.

Some of those that everybody should use are:

Ctrl + C to copy a cell (with format too)

Ctrl + V to paste the cell that you copied

Ctrl + X to cut the cell (instead of copying it, you remove it from its cell to paste it in another cell)

Ctrl + to insert a column or row (selecting the column or row previously)

Ctrl – to delete a column or row (selecting the column or row previously)

Surely with these shortcuts you can move a little faster. But there are more that are quite useful.

WHY DO YOU NEED TO LEARN TO USE CHARTS?

Charts are, by excellence, the way to communicate quantitative information in the business world, in non-profit organizations, in schools, in governmental organizations, in health areas, in sports, etc.

It's very simple, if you want to effectively communicate your numerical data, you need to master the Excel Charts. That includes the use of tables and the correct positioning of them, the selection of the data that you need, the Chart Type selection and the modification of the parameters of the chart.

Also, it becomes necessary that you

learn to discover what a chart wants to "tell you". Correctly analyzing the data in a chart usually leads to better decisions.

If you want to make better decisions in your job or company, it is very likely that becoming an Excel Charts and Graphs Champion will benefit you

I WOULD LOVE TO READ YOUR COMMENTS

Before you go, I would like to tell you Thank You for buying my book. It is my wish that the information you obtained in **EXCEL VLOOKUP NINJA** helps you in your job or business, and that you can have greater productivity and more free time to use it in the activities that you like the most.

I realize that you could have chosen among several other Excel books but you chose **EXCEL VLOOKUP NINJA** and you invested your time and effort. I am honored to have the opportunity to help you.

I'd like to ask you a small favor. <u>**Could you take a minute or two and leave a Review of EXCEL VLOOKUP NINJA on Amazon?**</u>

This feedback will be very appreciated

and will help me continue to write more courses that help you and a lot more people.

Share your comments with me and other readers

ABOUT THE AUTHOR

Henry E. Mejia is passionate about progress and goal achieving, he also loves to run and exercise. He works in the insurance industry and likes to invest in the stock market. While doing that, he devotes some time to create Excel written courses like this one, in order to help people to achieve their professional goals.

Henry also realized that the vast majority of people use a lot of their work time in front of the computer. That time could be used in more productive or more enjoyable activities, only if people knew how to use Excel a little better.

The goal of Henry's books is to open the door for workers and business owners to use Excel more efficiently, so they can have more and better growth opportunities, progress and free time.

www.ingramcontent.com/pod-product-compliance
Lightning Source LLC
La Vergne TN
LVHW051704050326
832903LV00032B/4006